Paragon Visu

Mechanical, Spatial & Abstract Reasoning

by

Craig Ma

GW00771911

Suitable for:

Police Force

Fire and Rescue Service

Ambulance Service

Defence Forces

Government Departments

Mining and Resources

Universities

High Schools

Mechanics in Motion Software Available
from: www.paragontraining.com.au

Copyright ©20.... ....gon Visual Education Pty Ltd.
C4, 58
Newcastle Street
PERTH WA 6000
Australia

ph/fax +61 8 9227 5125
email craig@paragontraining.com.au

ISBN: 978-1-925209-36-5
Published by Vivid Publishing
P.O. Box 948, Fremantle
Western Australia 6959
www.vividpublishing.com.au

Cataloguing-in-Publication data is available from the National Library of Australia

To order further copies of the print edition, find out more about the book
or contact the author, please visit: www.paragontraining.com.au

Subjects include: Mechanical Reasoning, Spatial Reasoning, Abstract Reasoning, Aptitude
Testing, Psychometric Testing

Production: Layout, typesetting, and animations were by Katamanti Media. The book was prepared using Adobe® InDesign®.

About the Production Team

Craig MacKellar B.A. (Training & Development), Cert IV Assessment & Workplace Training is an experienced trainer, instructor and author and the Managing Director of Paragon Corporate Training.

Craig was an officer in the Western Australian Police Service for fifteen years and a WA Police Academy Instructor from 1992 – 1995. Craig has continued to work closely with police, emergency, and other public services in WA through his Security and Training businesses, as well as providing training to the private sector. Paragon Corporate Training is a Registered Training Organisation. Craig has authored a number of successful training books in the fields of numerical reasoning, language use, and mechanical, spatial and abstract reasoning.

Jill Luha B.A., Grad. Cert. Ed., Grad. Dip. Curric. & Ed. Tech., Grad. Dip. Computing is an experienced teacher, trainer and instructional designer.

Jill has held posts as Senior Tutor in Educational Computing in the Faculty of Education at the Western Australian Institute of Technology (now Curtin University), and Teacher in charge of Computing at All Saints' College, Bull Creek, Western Australia. She has written several successful computer training books, which are in widespread use throughout Australia, and contributed to the instructional design of a videodisk training project.

Tony Luha B.Sc., D. Phil., Grad. Dip. Ed. (Higher & Further) is an experienced lecturer and trainer.

Tony worked as a university lecturer in biochemistry, and industrial trainer in the U.K. before coming to Australia. Since arriving in WA, he has held posts as Education Officer (Educational Computing) in the Education Department of WA (Now Department of Training), and as lecturer in Educational Computing at Curtin University. He has also held a contract post at Curtin University as Lecturer in On-Line Learning Development.

Jill and Tony retired from their publishing business in 2002 to pursue interests in multimedia through their new business Katamanti Media. The chance to work with Paragon Visual Education and Paragon Corporate Training, and contribute to Paragon's fine product range has been a fulfilling and worthwhile experience.

Contents

Preface

A note from the author

The specific industry skills identified as essential for entry into the various emergency services can be elusive for many people. Yet, the skills required to demonstrate a sound aptitude for learning are inherent in us all. What often remains dormant is the commitment to take on a challenge. It is the challenge and commitment that inspires people to do great things.

I have heard people say that you cannot prepare for these types of tests but that is simply not true. You can learn strategies and techniques to apply to these types of tests and actually score higher than you would have done without any preparation.

In most cases where an applicant has failed a general ability test or physical assessment, they were unprepared.

People's literacy and numeric skills, test taking skills, behavioural skills as well as fitness level, all diminish through lack of use or practice. Many adults, especially adults of indigenous and non-English speaking background, may not have had the opportunity to gain the skills, such as numerical problem solving and work place English, demanded by industry as pre-requisite for employment.

This book is not about making you smarter but rather using your intelligence in a better way; being smarter about how you approach abstract problems for example.

The book provides a generous amount of questions for mechanical, abstract and spatial reasoning. The questions are all very similar to psychometric tests used throughout the world.

Craig MacKellar
BA VET (Vocational Educational Development)

The competitiveness factor

Selection for that special job or position may be partly based on the highest scores over the entire selection process. This is called norm referencing. We discuss this later on in the book. It may not be good enough to pass in each test area. You may need to be competitive with the front-runners, in all areas.

Paragon Visual Education's 'Mechanical, Spatial and Abstract Reasoning' book has been developed to help you become super competitive in general aptitude tests involving these disciplines.

This program will:

❖   Bridge the gap between your existing knowledge and skills; and the skills and knowledge required to meet the selection criteria for the police, ambulance, prison and fire & rescue services.

❖   Allow graduates to perform to their full potential and therefore reflect a sound and competitive aptitude for learning.

❖   Focus on long term retention and competent application of knowledge and skills in a workplace context.

Introduction

Learning Outcomes: Skills you can apply after completing this text

This text provides an overview of key principles associated with psychometric testing relating to spatial and abstract thought.

By applying the principles outlined in the examples to other abstract problems the candidate should more readily identify rules and relationships.

Our aim is to facilitate the following learning outcomes.

❖ **Identify individual elements** within a group of elements;

❖ **Identify a rule** connecting a set of figures;

❖ **Complete a number of test questions** by applying a rule connecting a set of figures;

❖ **Apply techniques aimed at increasing the speed at which logical rules are generated** (the faster a person generates solutions, the higher the probability of a correct answer—in a given period of time);

❖ **Increase the number of elements a person can keep track of in responding to an item (span capacity).** Someone with a larger span capacity than someone else can take into account more figures without making errors and hence has a larger probability of a correct answer.

Assessment criteria

The assessments at the end of this program are intended to measure general intelligence as demonstrated by the ability to see relationships and to solve problems presented in a spatial or abstract context. The tests in this book utilise a number of types of item which are judged to contribute to an assessment of the general ability factor as described by *Spearman. (see page 7)*

Norms

Did you know that your assessment relates to your percentile ranking, not percentage scores?

Percentile rankings relate to how your score compares to others who have completed the same test.

For example when dealing with percentages, a score of 17 out of 34 would mean that the candidate got 50% of the questions correct.

When dealing in *percentiles* a score of 17 out of 34 may equate to *80 percentile*. This means that 20 % of the candidates who did the test got a better mark than 17; *80% of the candidates* got a mark lower than 17.

About Progressive Matrices

Spatial and Abstract Reasoning ability is a key element in identifying a person's general intelligence. That is why the vast majority of psychometric tests will have a component that relates to abstract and spatial reasoning.

> 'The Standard Progressive Matrices is a test on non-verbal reasoning ability. It was developed from work carried out in Britain in the 1930s (Penrose and Raven, 1936). It was designed as a measure of Spearman's g factor (see illustration on page 7). This factor is assumed to underlie general reasoning ability and to account for the strong positive relationship between all measures of cognitive functioning. Spearman (1927) identified two distinct processes in measures of **g: eductive ability, or the ability to educe relationships and correlates (i.e. inferring a general rule from specific instances and recognising specific instances from the general rule); and reproductive ability, which is based on recall of acquired information.**

The Progressive Matrices provide a measure of eductive ability or fluid intelligence which is relatively independent of specific learning acquired in a particular cultural or educational context. The test loads heavily on the g factor, and has been recognised as one of the purest single measures of g available. (Jensen, 1980)'.

Australian Council of Educational Research

Thurstone and Spearman's Concept of General Intelligence

The diagram below illustrates the concept of general intelligence incorporating *Thurstone and Spearman's* theories. The so-called seven primary mental abilities provide a sound model to describe the various disciplines and thought processes that contribute to a person's general intelligence.

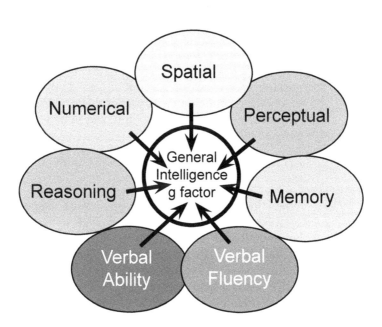

Raven Progressive Matrices

The Raven Progressive Matrices (RPM) test is a widely-known intelligence test in many research and applied settings. In each item of this test, the candidate is asked to find a rule connecting a set of figures, and to complete this set according to the rule.

The goal of research is to decompose performance on this test; it is assumed that, essentially, two distinct abilities are relevant in RPM items. The first one is the speed at which logical rules are identified. The faster a person generates solutions, the higher their probability of a correct answer (in a given period of time). The second is the number of elements a person can keep track of in responding to an item (span capacity). Someone with a larger span capacity than someone else has a larger probability of a correct answer.

Hints for completing Spatial and Abstract Reasoning tests

1. The test is generally timed so you cannot afford to spend too much time on any one particular problem. You do not lose marks for an incorrect answer and each question is only worth 1 mark so you don't get extra marks for completing the harder problems. Do as many as you can within the time limit. Set your watch and manage your time carefully.

2. Do not leave any answers blank on multiple choice tests.

3. When looking at a matrix with lots of shapes and symbols, some running vertically and some running horizontally, it is tempting to look at all of the elements that make up the symbols and shapes that are characteristic of the rule or principle. People with an above average span capacity may be able to identify the rule or principle fairly quickly by doing this, however most people may find breaking the shapes and symbols down to their individual elements an easier way of solving these matrices.

Our brain is a marvelous phenomenon, yet the average person when shown ten objects on a table for about 10 seconds, can only remember about 7 of the items when asked to write them down on a list.

When dealing with matrices you may find it easier to identify the rule by breaking the task up into individual elements and establish what is happening to each individual element. If you do this for all of the elements that make up the matrix you should be able to work out the rule/principle associated with the question. As you become more confident you can increase your span capacity to include more than one element at a time in your analysis.

Obviously the quicker you identify the rule and apply it to the matrix, the more questions you are likely to answer in the time frame and the higher probability of a competitive mark.

Good luck !!

Spatial Reasoning

Directions

In the tests that follow, you are presented with a matrix of shapes. Your task is to recognise patterns in the matrix that run across the rows and down the columns and thereby identify the shape or shapes missing from the bottom right position of the matrix.

There are four examples, with written explanations, to help you. Examples 2 and 4 illustrate one common principle of spatial reasoning matrices: i.e. each element appears twice and twice only both across the rows or down the columns.

These tests differ from real-world tests only in that you can work them at your own pace. In a typical aptitude test there will be a strict time limit.

Read through and understand the examples and then move on to work the questions.

Example 1

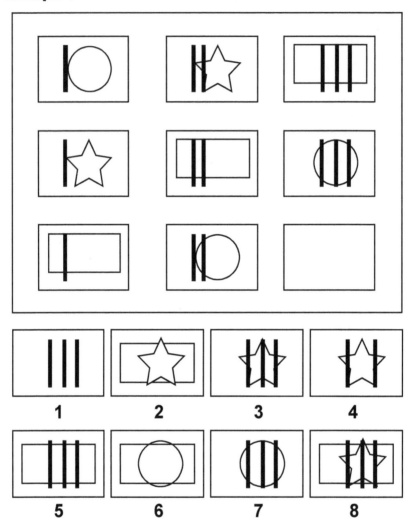

Explanation: The **elements** that make up example 1 are as follows:

Circle, Star, Rectangle, Solid lines and Quantity (1 to 3)

Looking at the top row from left to right we have a **circle**, **star** and **rectangle**. The middle row from left to right shows a **star**, **rectangle** and **circle** and the bottom row from left to right shows a **rectangle**, and a **circle**, so therefore a star is needed as the missing shape. If you look at the columns from left to right you will notice that the solid line is going up in quantity (1—2—3).

Our answer therefore is a Star with 3 vertical solid lines (No. 3).

Example 2

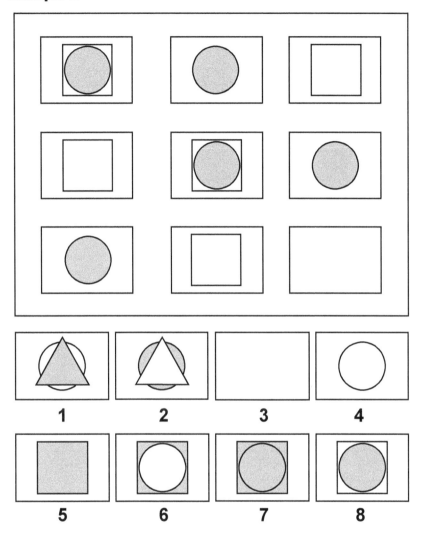

Explanation: The **elements** that make up example 2 are as follows:

Square, Circle, Shading and Quantity.

Each element appears twice, and twice only, either across the columns from left to right or down the rows from top to bottom.

In the top row the **left frame** is made up of the two elements from the middle and right frames. The **centre frame** in the middle row is made up of the left and right elements and the **right frame** in the bottom row is made up of the elements in the left and centre frames.

i.e. one frame + one frame = the other frame

Our answer is a shaded circle inside a clear square (No. 8).

Example 3

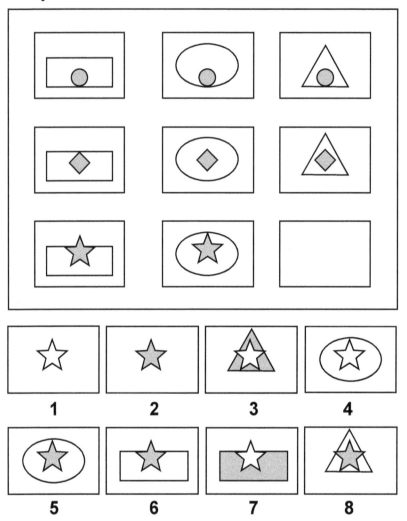

Explanation: The **elements** that make up example 3 are as follows:

Shaded circle, Shaded diamond, Shaded star, Rectangle, Oval, Triangle and **Quantity** (3 of each element).

Looking at the **shaded circle** in the top row going from left to right, you will notice it appears across the entire row. Looking at the **shaded diamond** in the middle row, you will notice it appears across the entire row. The same can be said about the **shaded star**. Looking at the other elements, that is, the **rectangle, oval and triangle**, you will notice that they run the length of the columns from left to right respectively.

Our answer therefore is the shaded star in the triangle (No. 8).

Example 4

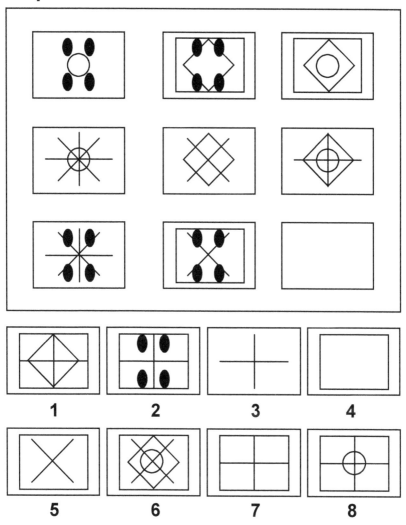

Explanation: the **elements** that make up example 4 are as follows:

A set of four black dots, Circle, Diamond, Rectangle, Heavy black diagonal lines, Light horizontal and vertical lines (cross) and Quantity (usually 3 of each element although sometimes only 2).

Either by looking at the columns from left to right or alternatively by choosing the rows from top to bottom you should notice that each element appears twice and twice only across either the columns or rows. It doesn't matter which way you look at it you should still arrive at the same answer.

Our answer therefore is a cross inside a rectangle (No. 7).

Q1

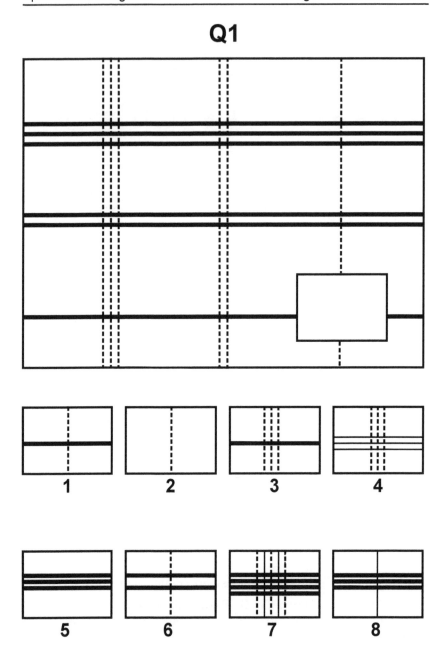

Q2

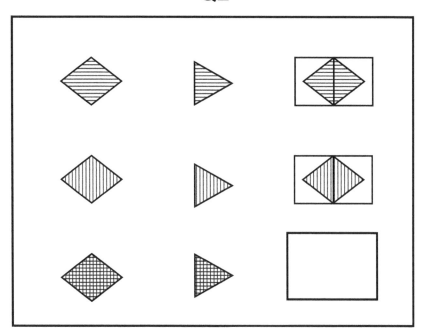

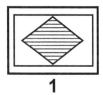
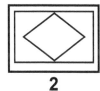

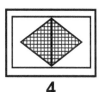

1   **2**   **3**   **4**

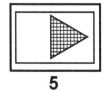
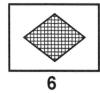
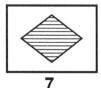
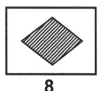

5   **6**   **7**   **8**

Q3

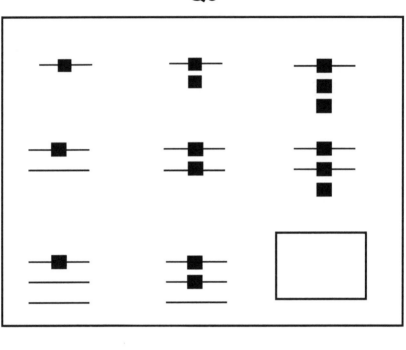

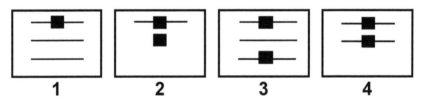

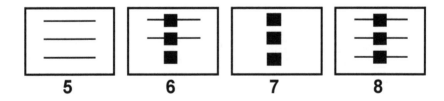

Q4

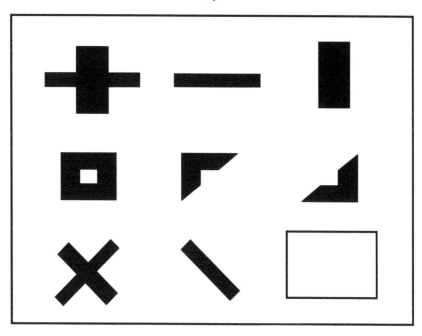

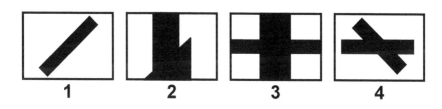

| 1 | 2 | 3 | 4 |

| 5 | 6 | 7 | 8 |

Q5

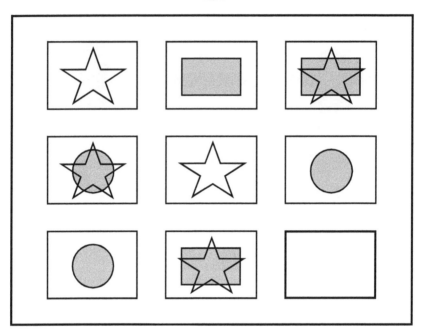

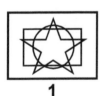
1

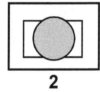
2

3

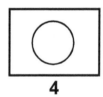
4

5

6

7

8

Q6

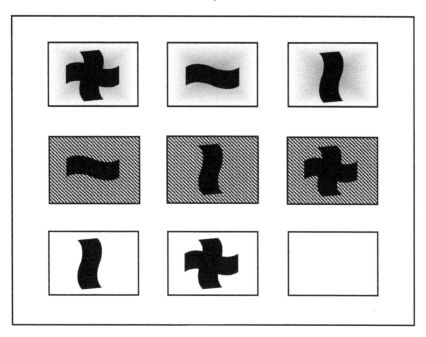

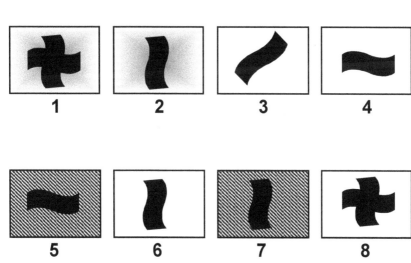

Q7

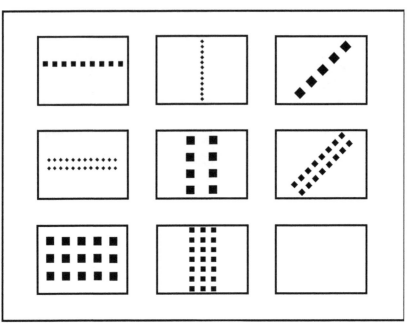

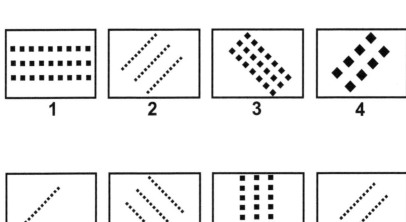

Q8

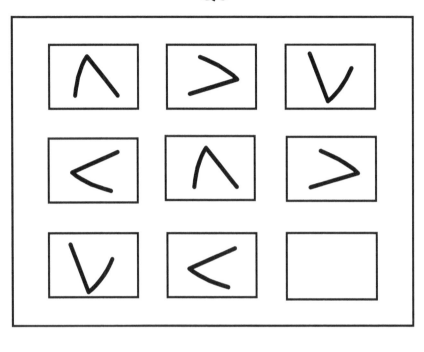

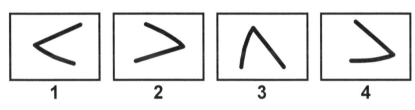

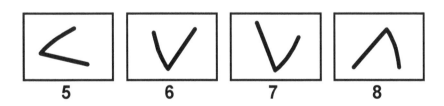

Q9

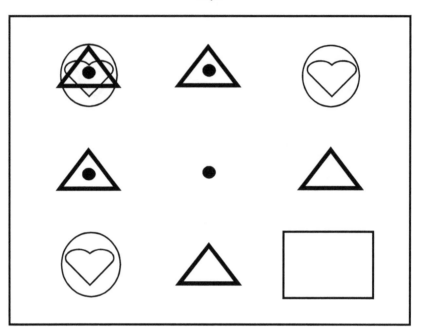

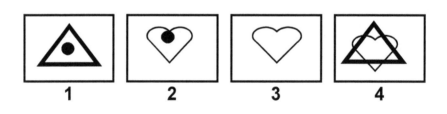

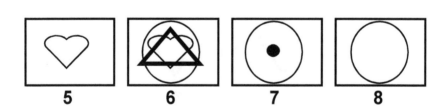

Q10

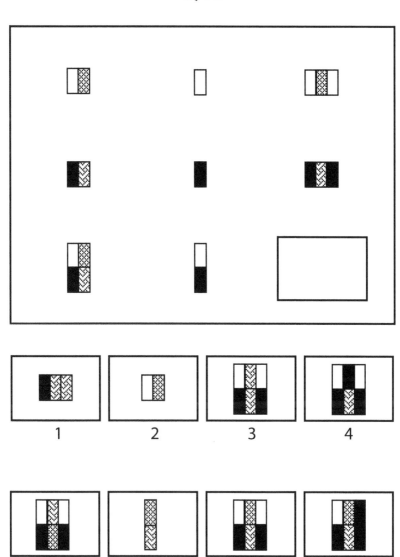

Q11

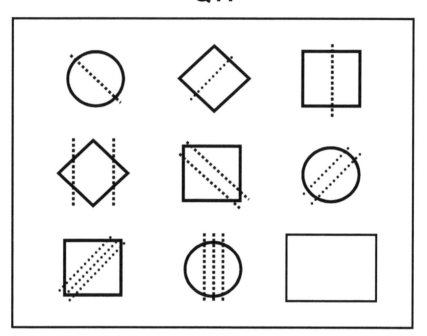

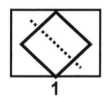
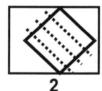
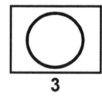
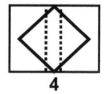

1   **2**   **3**   **4**

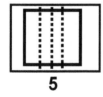
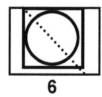
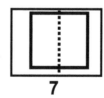
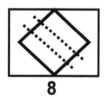

5   **6**   **7**   **8**

Q12

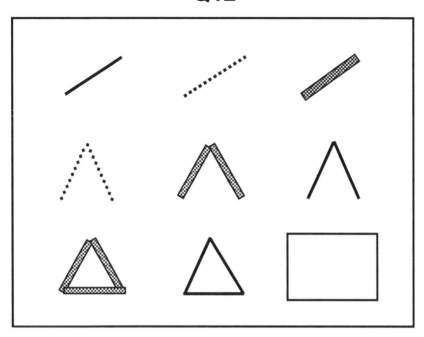

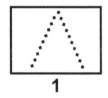
1

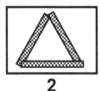
2

3

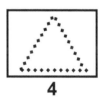
4

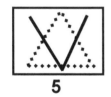
5

6

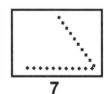
7

8

Q13

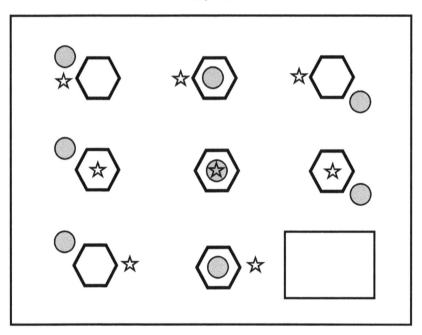

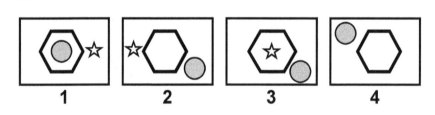

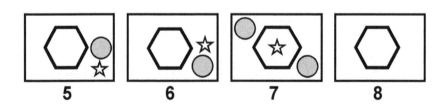

Q14

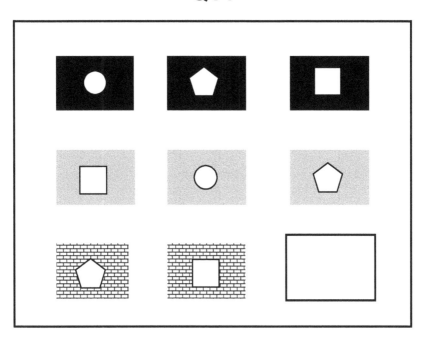

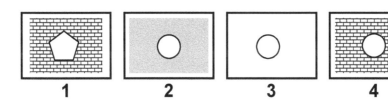

1   2   3   4

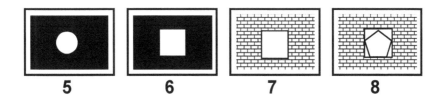

5   6   7   8

Q15

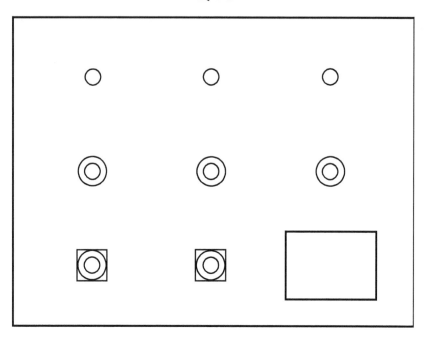

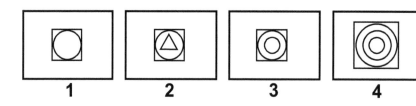

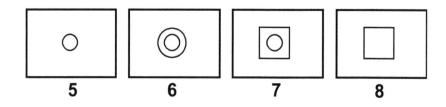

Q16

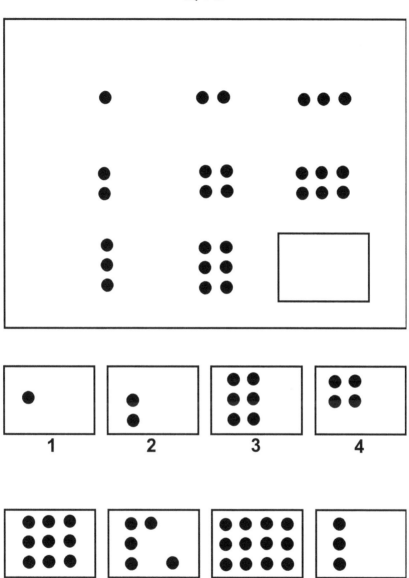

Q17

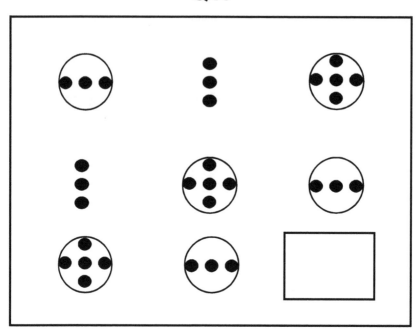

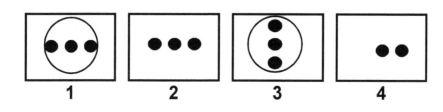

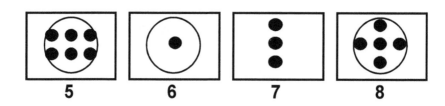

Q18

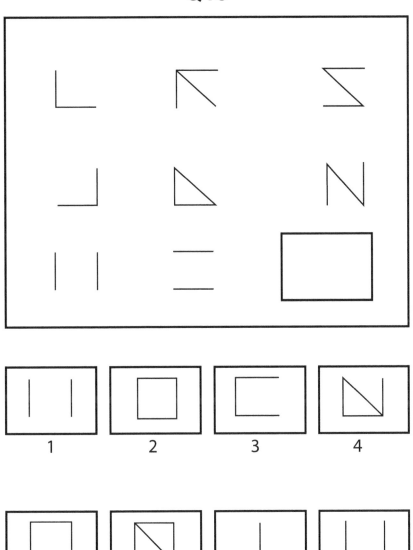

Q19

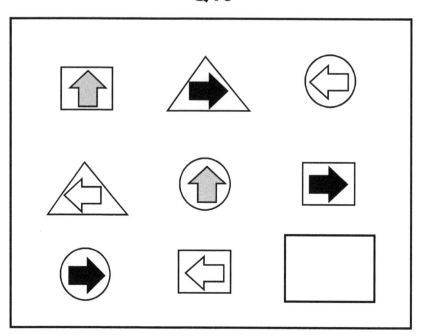

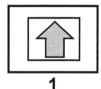			
1	**2**	**3**	**4**

5	**6**	**7**	**8**

Q20

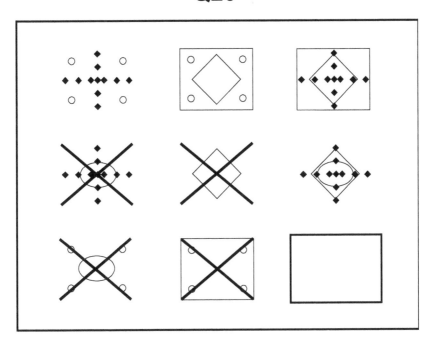

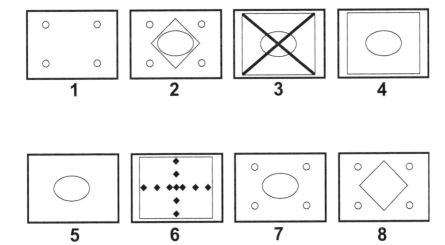

Q21

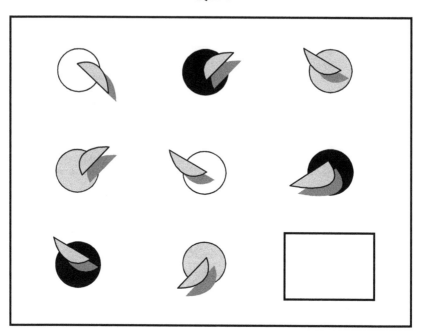

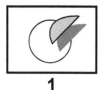
1

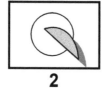
2

3

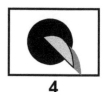
4

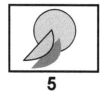
5

6

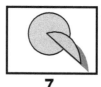
7

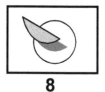
8

Q22

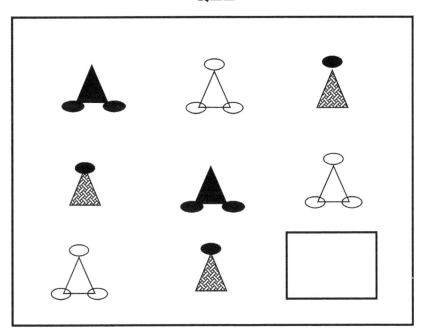

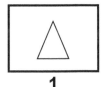
1

2

3

4

5

6

7

8

Q23

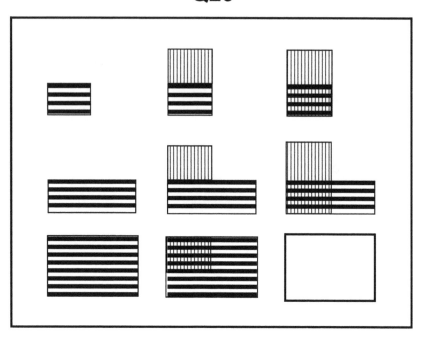

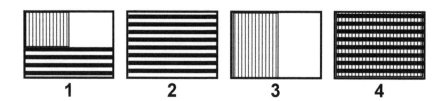

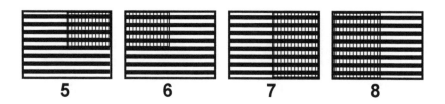

Q24

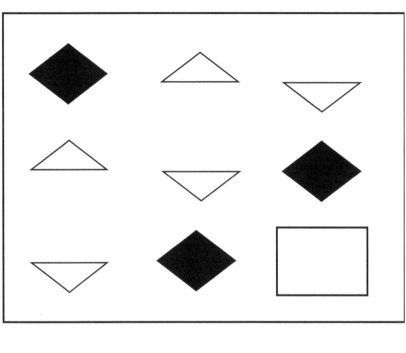

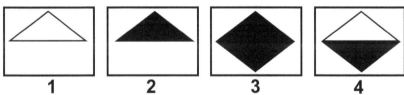

1   2   3   4

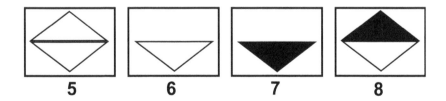

5   6   7   8

Q25

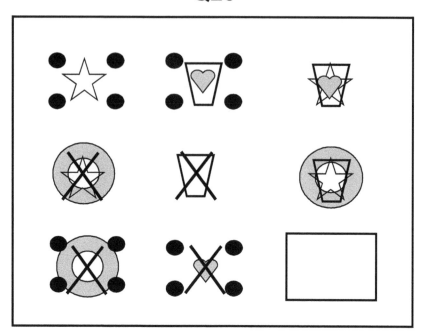

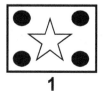
1

2

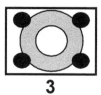
3

4

5

6

7

8

Q26

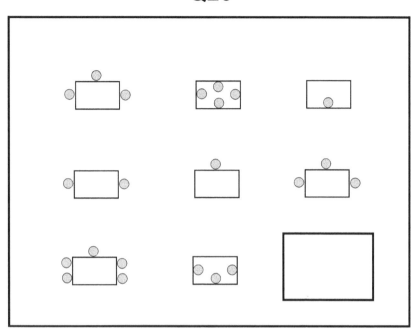

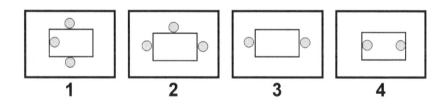

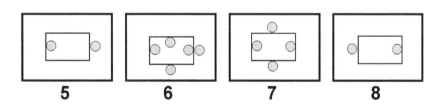

Q27

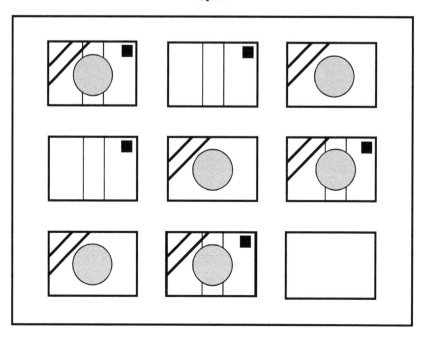

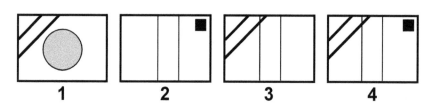

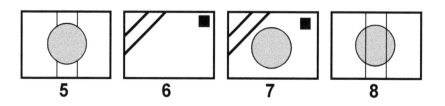

Q28

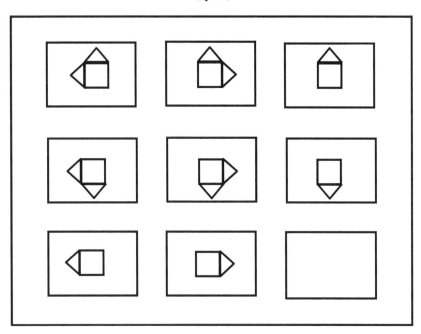

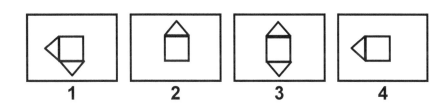

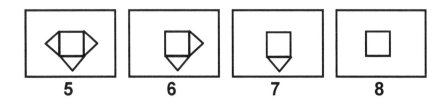

Q29

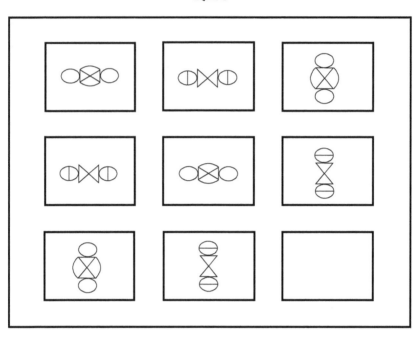

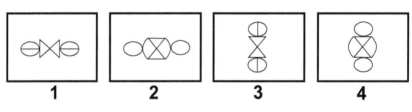

1   2   3   4

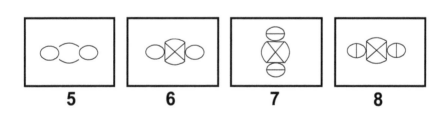

5   6   7   8

Q30

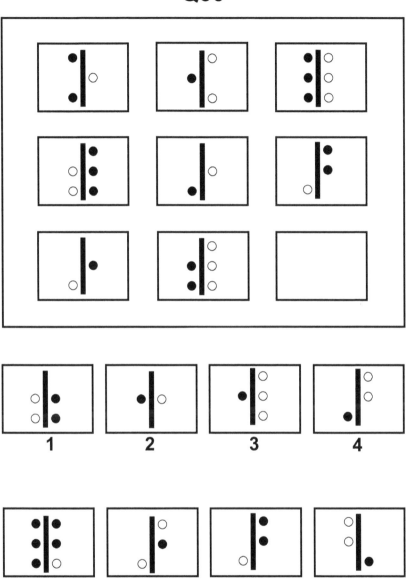

Q31

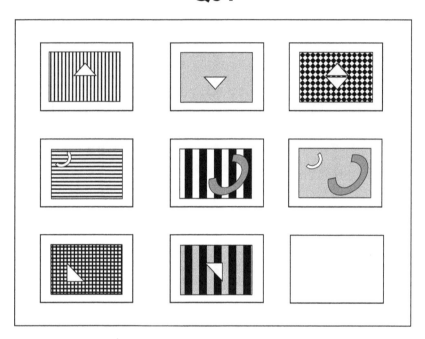

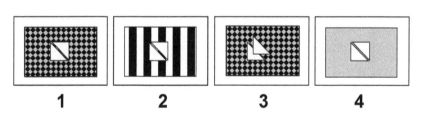

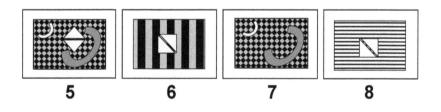

Q32

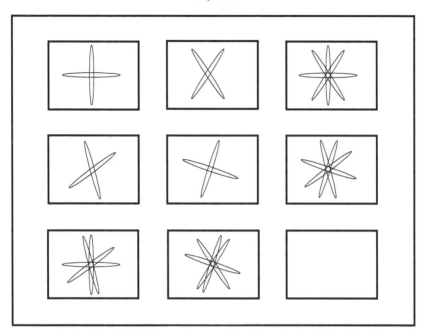

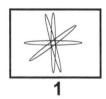

1

2

3

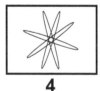

4

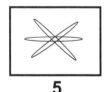

5

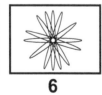

6

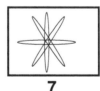

7

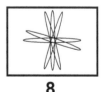

8

Q33

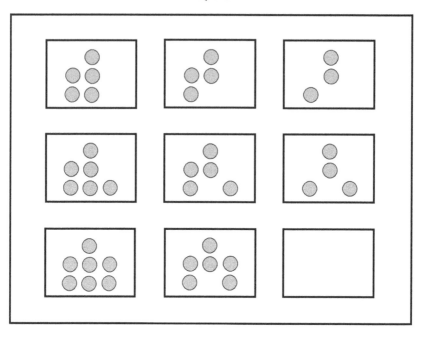

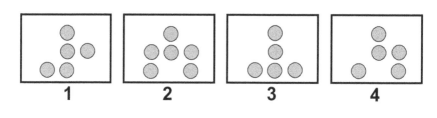

1   2   3   4

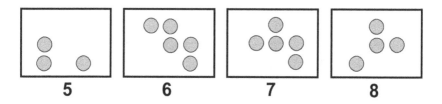

5   6   7   8

Q34

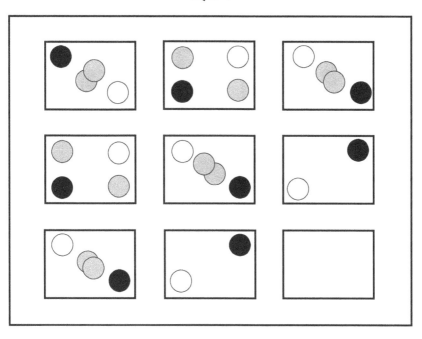

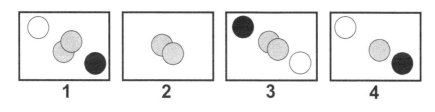

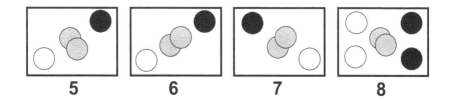

Q35

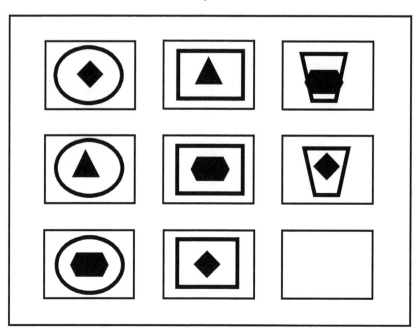

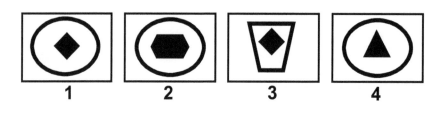

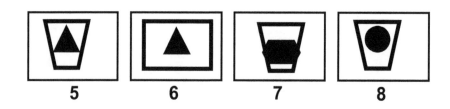

Q36

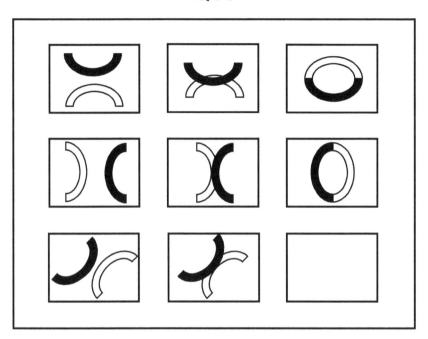

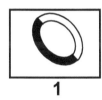

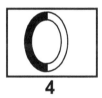

1   **2**   **3**   **4**

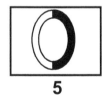
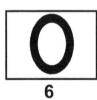
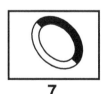

5   **6**   **7**   **8**

Q37

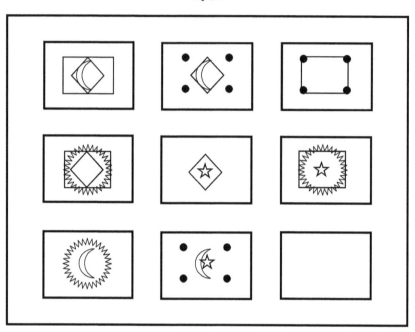

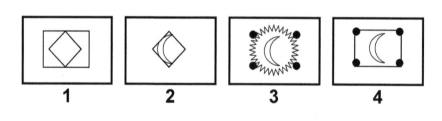

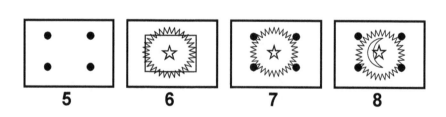

Q38

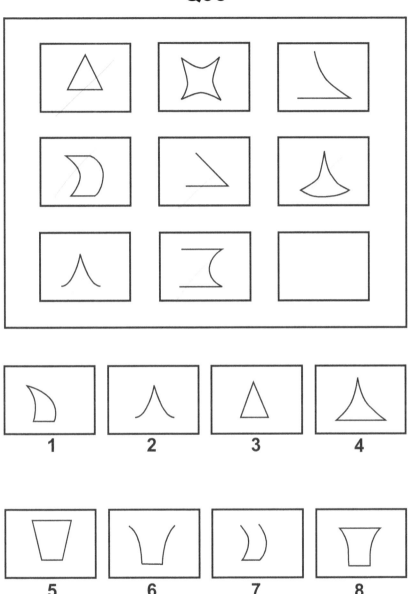

Q39

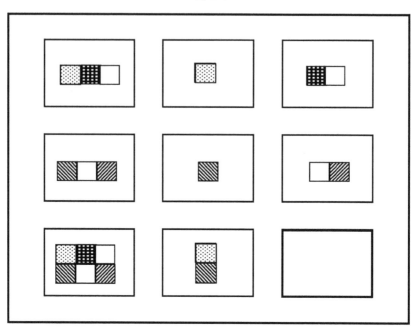

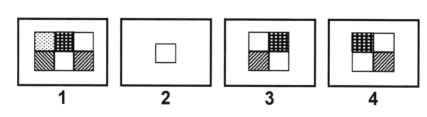

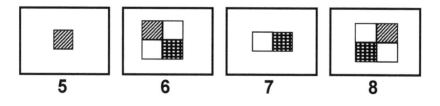

Q40

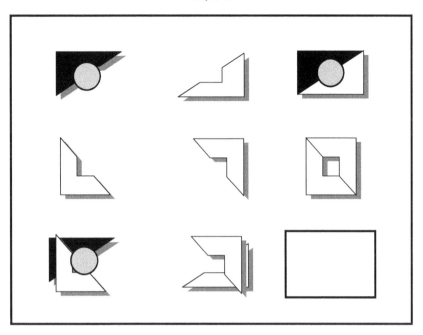

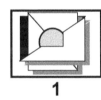

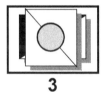
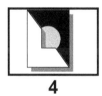

1　　　　**2**　　　　**3**　　　　**4**

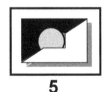

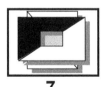
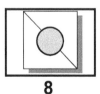

5　　　　**6**　　　　**7**　　　　**8**

Abstract Reasoning

Directions

In the following test you will see rows of patterns or symbols like those below. Each row across the page is one problem. You are to circle either **A, B, C, D or E** from the choices available on the right side of the page. You are to find out which one of the Answer figures would be the next (or the fifth one) in the series of Problem figures. Here are two examples:

Example 1

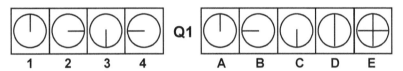

In this example note that the lines are rotating in a clockwise direction by 90 degrees as they move from frame 1 to frame 2 and so on. Therefore, with this principle/rule in mind the correct answer would have to be A. The line has moved back to its original starting point having moved a complete 360 degrees in a clockwise direction, moving 90 degrees at a time.

The answer is **(A)**

Example 2

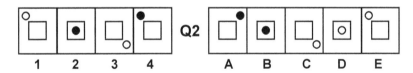

In this example, note that the circle is alternating from clear to shaded to clear, back to shaded. Therefore the answer needs to contain a clear circle. You will also notice that the circle is moving from top left corner to centre, to lower right corner back to the left corner again. Therefore our answer needs to have a clear circle positioned in the middle of the square.

The answer is **(D)**.

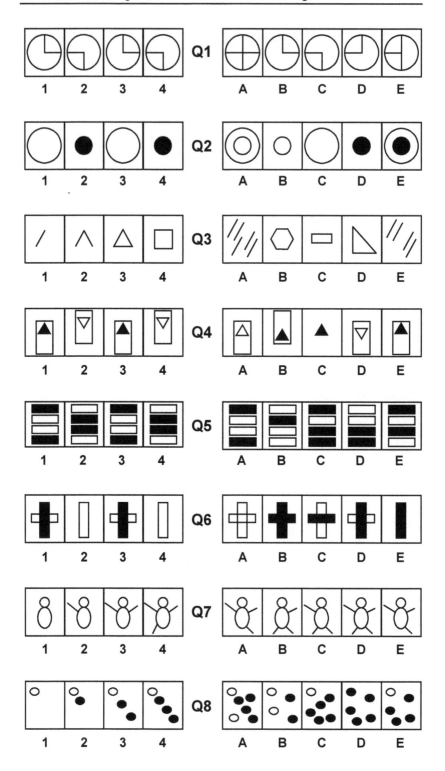

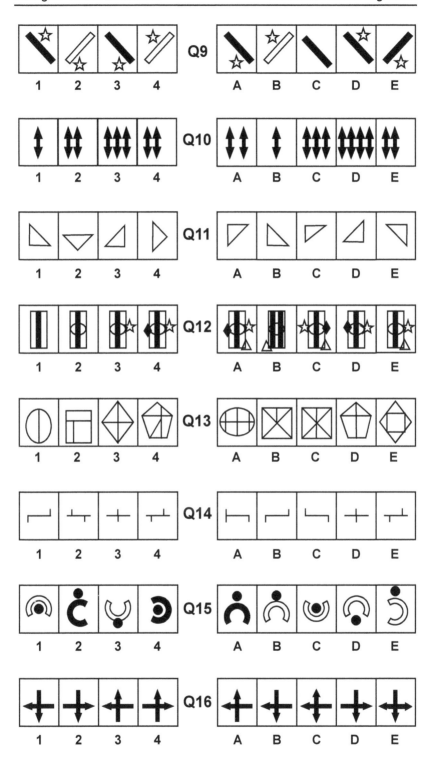

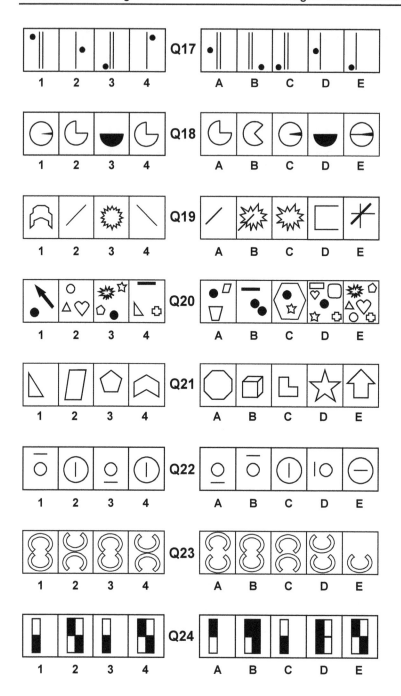

Mechanical Reasoning

Directions

These tests examine your ability to understand mechanical concepts. There are 32 questions in the first test and 20 questions in the second. Your task is to read each question and choose the best answer from the options provided. There are 4 alternatives to choose from.

For these tests, you need to understand what a pivot is. A pivot is a pin or axle around which a lever or wheel can turn. A **fixed pivot** is a pin or axle around which a lever or wheel can turn, but the **fixed pivot itself does not move position**. A **non-fixed pivot** is also a pin or axle around which a lever or wheel can turn, but the **non-fixed pivot itself can move** its **position**.

A fixed pivot is indicated throughout these tests by a black dot, and a non-fixed pivot is indicated by a clear dot, as shown in the example below:

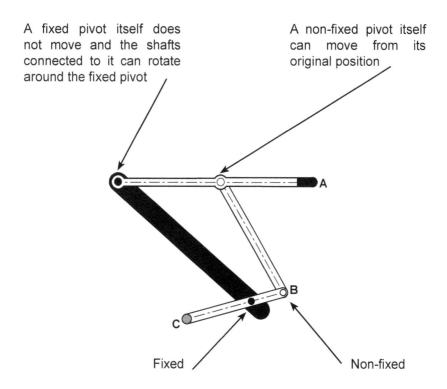

A fixed pivot itself does not move and the shafts connected to it can rotate around the fixed pivot

A non-fixed pivot itself can move from its original position

Fixed

Non-fixed

Q1 Wheels W and X are each 6 centimetres across. Wheels Y and Z are each 3 centimetres across. When W makes one complete turn, Z will make

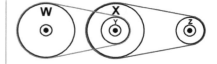

A   one complete turn

B   two complete turns

C   three complete turns

D   four complete turns

Q2 If handle A is pushed upwards in the direction of the arrow

A   end C will move down and end B will move up

B   end C will move up and end B will move down

C   end B will move up and end C will move up

D   end B will move down and end C will move down

Q3 If wheel W turns clockwise as indicated by the arrow, Z will

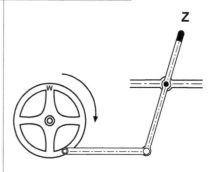

A   move to the left only

B   move to the right only

C   will not move at all as the mechanism is unworkable

D   move to and fro

Q4 If wheel A turns anticlockwise as indicated by the arrow, D will

A turn anticlockwise

B turn clockwise

C turn to and fro

D jam the mechanism

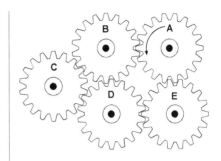

Q5 A and B are blocks attached to the cord which runs around this vertical system of wheels. If the cord is pulled to the left, as indicated by the arrow, how will A and B move?

A A goes up and B to the right

B A goes down and B to the right

C A goes down and B to the left

D A goes up and B to the left

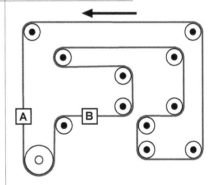

Q6 If handle H is pulled down, as indicated by the arrow, how will the hook at the end of non-fixed pivot L move?

A hook will move straight up and closer to L

B hook will move right only and remain same distance from L

C hook will move left but remain the same distance from L

D hook will move right, then left and closer to L

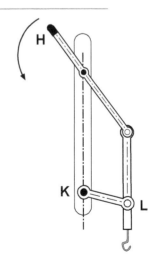

Q7 If handle A is pulled down, as indicated by the arrow, how will B move?

A B will remain in a fixed position

B B will move to the left and up

C B will move to the right and up

D B will move to and fro

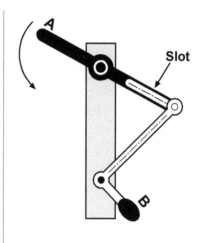

Q8 Wheel Z turns anticlockwise, as shown by the arrow, and drives wheel Y. A connecting rod attached to wheel Y moves in a slot. Will non fixed pivot P move

A to and fro with pauses

B to the right and jam

C to the left and jam

D to and fro continuously

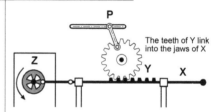

Q9 In this 5-storey factory, the motor on the ground floor uses belts A, B, C and D to drive conveyors on the 1st, 2nd, 3rd and 4th floors. If the conveyors on the 1st and 2nd floors are turning but the conveyors on the 3rd and 4th floors are not, which of the belts is most likely to have broken?

A A

B B

C C

D D

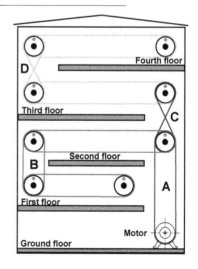

Q10 If handle X is pulled down as indicated by the arrow, Z (hook) will

A   move left and closer to Y

B   move left and remain the same distance from Y

C   move right and further away from Y

D   remain in its position

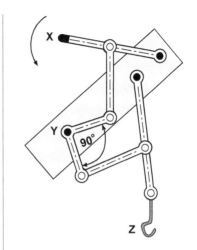

Q11 If handle X is pulled down, as indicated by the arrow, W (hook) will

A   remain in its position

B   move right and further away from Y

C   move left and closer to Y

D   move left and further away from Z

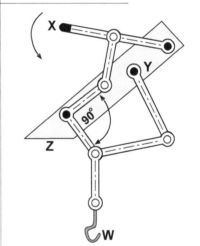

Q12 If handle A is pulled down as indicated by the arrow, B will move

A   up and closer to pivot Y

B   down and further away from pivot Y

C   up and remain the same distance from Y

D   down and further away from X

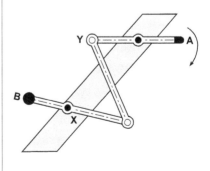

Q13 If wheels X and Y move in the direction of the arrows, A will

A move to the right first and then to the left in pauses

B move to the left first and then to the right continuously

C not move at all as the mechanism would jam

D move to the right first and then to the left continuously

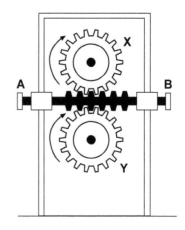

Q14 If the belt driven by the motor is travelling anticlockwise as shown by the arrow, then how many wheels in total will be turning clockwise?

A one

B two

C three

D four

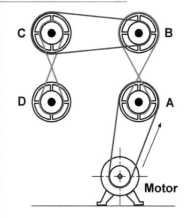

Q15 Wheels B and C have pins which fit into the slots in wheel A. Both wheels B and C turn in the direction of the arrows and drive wheel A. Wheel A will

A turn anticlockwise continuously

B turn clockwise continuously

C turn to and fro

D not operate as C and B are opposing forces

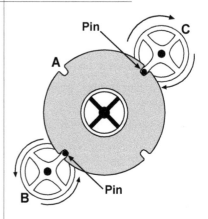

Q16 Block A is supported by springs X and Z. Spring Z is three times as strong as spring X. If both screws are turned at the same speed in the directions shown by the arrows, towards which point will block A move?

A   X

B   Y

C   P

D   Q

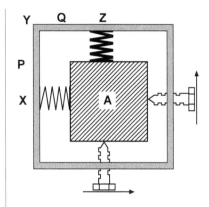

Q17 If wheel A turns in the direction as shown by the arrow, which one of the following is true?

A   D, C, and B all turn in the same direction

B   D and C turn in opposite directions

C   A and B turn in the same direction

D   A and B turn in opposite directions

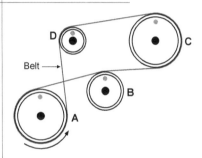

Q18 X and Y are blocks attached to the cord which runs around this system of wheels. If the cord is pulled in the direction of the arrow until each block passes its first wheel, then which of the following is true?

A   X to the right then down, Y to the right then up and left

B   X to the left then up, Y to to the left then diagonally right

C   X to the right then down, Y to the right then up

D   X to the left then up, Y to the left then right

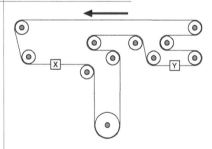

Q19 Wheels X, Y and Z can turn to and fro. If Z is turned clockwise, as shown by the arrow, then

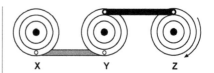

A   X and Y will both turn clockwise

B   X will turn clockwise and Y will turn anticlockwise

C   X and Y will both turn anticlockwise

D   X will turn anticlockwise and Y will turn clockwise

Q20 If handle J is pulled up, as shown by the arrow, how will M (hook) move?

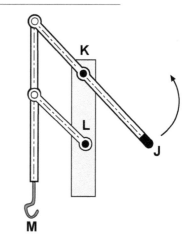

A   straight out to the left, further away from K

B   up to the left, further away from L

C   down to the left, further away from L

D   down and to the left, same distance from L

Q21 A, B and C are gears which turn on shafts and drive rods X and Y. When wheels A and C turn clockwise as shown by the arrows, rods X and Y will

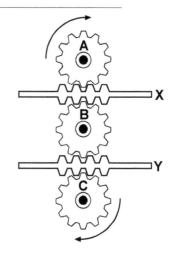

A   slide in opposite directions to each other

B   jam the mechanism

C   both slide to the right

D   both slide to the left

Q22 If the handle is pulled to the right as shown by the arrow, T will move

A   to the right, same distance from R

B   closer to the handle, further away from R

C   to the left and closer to R

D   closer to the handle, same distance from R

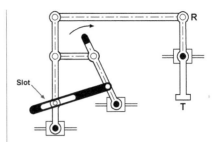

Q23 If the belt driven by the motor travels anticlockwise as shown by the arrow, then which of the following is true?

A   M and K turn in opposite directions and J and L turn in opposite directions

B   M and K turn in the same direction and J and K turn in the same direction

C   M and J turn in the same direction

D   L and K turn in the same direction

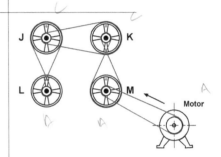

Q24 If the handle is pulled in the direction of the arrow, which mechanism out of J, K, L and M will act as a brake?

A   J

B   K

C   L

D   M

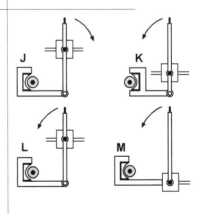

Q25 When S turns anticlockwise as shown by the arrow, it will drive wheels T and U

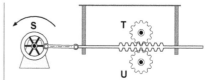

A   both clockwise to and fro

B   both anticlockwise continuously

C   both anticlockwise to and fro

D   T clockwise and U anticlockwise, to and fro

Q26 When handle S is pulled to the right as shown by the arrow, T will

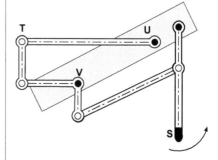

A   remain in its present position

B   move closer to V and closer to U

C   move closer to V, same distance from U

D   move further away from S and closer to U

Q27 When the motor drives wheels L, K and M, which one of the following statements is true?

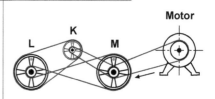

A   M and L will turn clockwise and K will turn anticlockwise

B   not work because L and M are opposing forces

C   not work because L and K are opposing forces

D   M and K will turn clockwise and L will turn anticlockwise

Q28 Wheel A has a pin near its edge. The pin engages in the slot in wheel B. When wheel A turns clockwise as shown, how will wheel B move?

A   the mechanism will jam

B   anticlockwise intermittently

C   to and fro

D   anticlockwise continuously

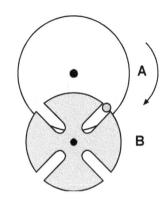

Q29 Wheels J and L turn as indicated by the arrows. Which of the following statements is true?

A   the mechanism would not work as J and K are opposing forces

B   all wheels turn anticlockwise except for M and L

C   J, K and L turn anticlockwise, M and L turn clockwise

D   only L turns clockwise

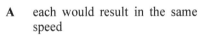

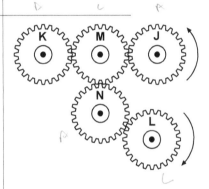

Q30 The motor drives the upper shaft at a constant speed. A, B and C are pairs of wheels attached to each shaft. To make the lower shaft turn the fastest, around which pair of wheels would a belt be attached?

A   each would result in the same speed

B   A

C   B

D   C

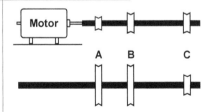

Q31 In this 5-storey building, the motor on the ground floor uses belts J, K, L and M to drive conveyor belts on the 1st, 2nd, 3rd and 4th floors. If the 2nd, 3rd and 4th floor conveyor belts are working but not the 1st floor, what is the most likely explanation?

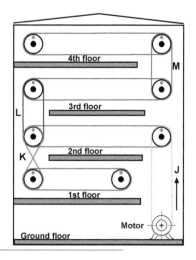

A   motor is not working

B   belt K is broken

C   belts K and L are broken

D   belts J and K are broken

Q32 Cam A turns clockwise at constant speed, and drives punch P through the levers shown. For each rotation of the cam, punch P will

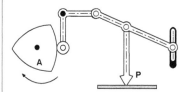

A   do nothing as the mechanism will jam

B   punch onto the plate three times

C   punch onto the plate just once

D   punch right through the plate just once

Mechanical Reasoning 2

Directions

This test examines your ability to understand mechanical concepts. There are 20 questions in this test. Your task is to read each question and choose the best answer from the options provided. There are 4 alternatives to choose from.

Some of the questions refer to fixed and non-fixed pivots. A fixed pivot is indicated throughout this test by a black dot, and a non-fixed pivot is indicated by a clear dot, as shown in the example below:

For a fuller explantion of fixed and non-fixed pivots, please refer to the Directions for Mechanical Reasoning 1 in the previous section.

A fixed pivot itself does not move and the shafts connected to it can rotate around the fixed pivot

A non-fixed pivot itself can move from its original position

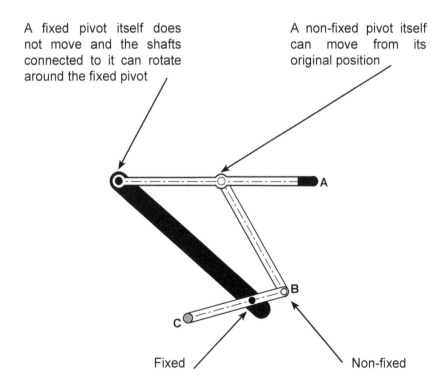

Fixed

Non-fixed

Q1 As pin P is hammered down, the fit of axle A to wheel W will become:

A tighter

B looser

C unchanged

D first looser then tighter

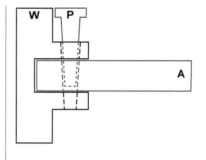

Q2 Identical floats have equal lead weights attached as shown. They are released into the liquids shown. After the floats come to rest, which container has the highest level of liquid?

A petrol

B sea water

C pure water

D all the same

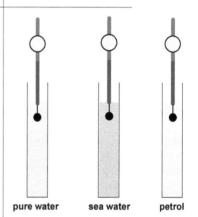

pure water   sea water   petrol

Q3 Weight W is placed on a plank which is supported by scales A and B. As W is moved from right to left along the plank, what will happen to the scale readings?

A A will increase and B will stay the same

B both A and B will stay the same

C A will increase and B will decrease

D A will decrease and B will increase

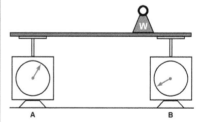

Q4 Which wheel will rotate the fastest?

A   A

B   B

C   C

D   all the same

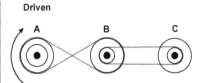

Q5 At which point is the pressure greatest?

A   A

B   B

C   C

D   all the same

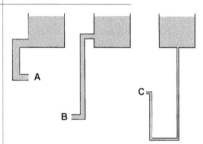

Q6 Which tree will fall to the right?

A   A

B   B

C   neither

D   both

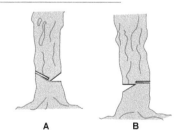

Q7 Which pendulum swings the fastest?

A   A

B   B

C   C

D   all the same

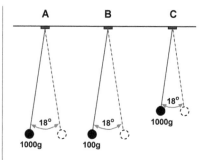

Q8 Wheel A is driven clockwise as shown. Which of the following statements is true?

A   wheel B will rotate continuously clockwise

B   wheel B will rotate continuously anticlockwise

C   the mechanism will jam

D   wheel B will rotate to and fro

Q9 Which switch or switches must be closed to light both globes?

A   A only

B   B only

C   C only

D   B and C

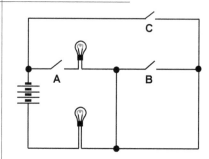

Q10 When cams X, Y and Z are driven about their fixed pivots, which rod will travel the greatest distance?

A   A

B   B

C   C

D   all the same

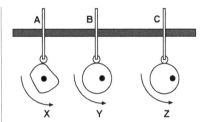

Q11 In this circuit which of the following statements is false?

A   operating switch A can light the lamp

B   operating switch B can light the lamp

C   operating both switches together can light the lamp

D   the lamp can be lit depending on the state of switches A and B

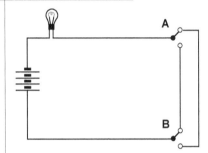

Q12 Which pair or pairs of magnets will attract?

A   A and B

B   all

C   A and C

D   B and D

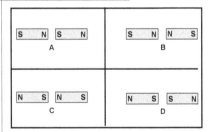

Q13 The circular glass tube is filled with liquid and heated from below as shown. Which of the following statements is true?

A the liquid will start to move either clockwise or anticlockwise at random

B the liquid will always start to move clockwise

C the liquid will always start to move anticlockwise

D the liquid will remain still

Q14 Shaft S is rotated clockwise as shown. Which of the following statements is true?

A A turns anticlockwise and B turns clockwise

B A turns clockwise and B turns anticlockwise

C both A and B turn clockwise

D the mechanism jams

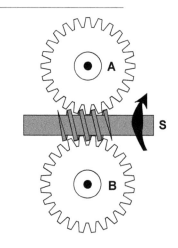

Q15 Each group of pulleys has wheels whose diameters are in the ratio 1:2:3. The top pulley wheels are all driven at the same speed of rotation. Which wheel will rotate the fastest?

A A

B B

C C

D D

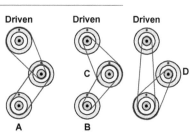

Q16 Pulley A turns clockwise as shown. Which of the following statements is true?

A   more pulleys turn clockwise than anticlockwise

B   more pulleys turn anticlockwise than clockwise

C   the same number of pulleys turn clockwise as anticlockwise

D   not all of the pulleys turn

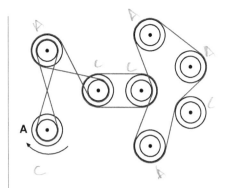

Q17 Which tyre has been used under-inflated?

A   A

B   B

C   C

D   D

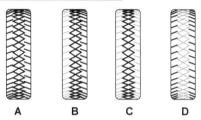

Q18 The circular plate is free to rotate around fixed pivot P. Three fixed threaded holes are in the plate below. In which hole should thumbscrew T be placed to give the circular plate the maximum possible movement?

A   A

B   B

C   C

D   either A or B

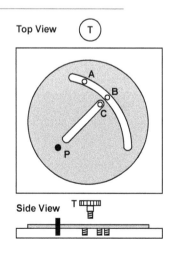

Q19 Rack A is pushed in the direction shown by the arrow. Which of the following statements is true?

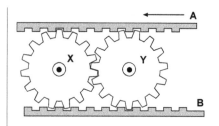

A   gears X and Y turn in the same direction

B   gears X and Y turn in opposite directions

C   rack B moves left to right

D   rack B does not move

Q20 A spring holds lever L against fixed pin P. Gear X drives gear Y. Which of the following statements is true?

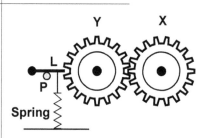

A   with a weak spring, gear X can turn clockwise

B   with a weak spring, gear X can turn anticlockwise

C   with a strong spring, gear X can turn clockwise

D   with a strong spring, gear X can turn anticlockwise.

Answers

Spatial Reasoning

Question	Answer and Explanation.	
1	(1)	Solid horizontal & 1 broken vertical intersecting in the middle.
2	(4)	Right column = rectangle + left column + middle column OR bottom row = top row + middle row
3	(8)	From left column to right column the black squares go up in sequence 1—2—3. And the horizontal lines are increasing in sequence 1—2—3 as we go down from top to bottom, so for our answer we need 3 black squares on 3 horizontal lines.
4	(1)	This principle is common throughout many spatial matrices. The shapes in the left column are made up of each of the individual elements from the middle and right columns. The element missing to make the diagonal cross illustrated at the bottom left is the element shown in ANSWER # 1. OR another way of looking at the matrix is to observe that each element appears in each row twice and twice only.
5	(8)	This principle is common throughout many spatial matrices. One picture in each row is made up of the other two pictures in the row. One picture in each column is made up of the other two pictures in the column. OR another way of looking at the matrix is to observe that each element appears in each column and row twice and twice only.
6	(4)	One picture in each row is made up of the other two pictures in the row.
7	(2)	Each row from left to right has a horizontal, vertical and diagonal line. Each line is made up of a different line style. Reading from left to right the columns go, horizontal—vertical—diagonal. Reading from top to bottom the number of lines increases from 1—2—3. We are missing the 3 diagonal lines in the right column made up of small diamonds.
8	(3)	From left to right across each row, the object is rotating clockwise 90 degrees each time. From top to bottom down each column, the object is rotating 90 degrees anticlockwise.

9	(6)	From left to right going across OR from top to bottom going down, each element appears twice only.
10	(7)	See principle as explained in ANSWER #5.
11	(2)	The missing shape is the diamond. The missing lines need to run diagonally from top left to bottom right. The quantity of lines is three.
12	(4)	Three different line styles; solid, dotted (small diamonds) & bar with dots. From top to bottom the quantity increases from 1—2—3. The elements that form our answer are comprised of 3 dotted lines (small diamonds) in the shape of a triangle.
13	(6)	The elements in this matrix consist of a shaded dot, a star and a shape (six sides). The shape is in all of them. The shaded dot is in the top left corner in the 1st column, in the centre cell in the middle column and in the bottom right corner in the left column. The star is in the left centre position in the top row, in the centre in the middle row and in the right centre position in the bottom row.
14	(4)	Missing elements are the brickwork background and circle.
15	(3)	Missing elements are fairly evident as you look at this from left to right OR top to bottom.
16	(5)	Top row + middle row = bottom row OR left column + middle column = right column.
17	(7)	Each element appears twice only down each column OR along each row.
18	(2)	As above
19	(5)	The missing elements are a triangle and an arrow. The missing arrow shape must be shaded grey, and must be pointing in the 'up' direction.
20	(4)	Each element appears twice only down each column OR across each row.
21	(2)	The circle needs to be clear. The grey "tab" is rotating 45 degrees anticlockwise as it is moving down the columns or across the rows.
22	(3)	Each row or column needs a triangle that is black, clear and patterned. In each row or column there will always be 1 black dot and 1 clear dot on top of the triangle, and 2 clear dots and 2 black dots at the bottom of the triangle. Another way of looking at it is each shape should appear 3 times in the matrix (1 in each row or column).

23	(8)	Element 1 (horizontal lines) is doubling in size from the top row to the middle row to the bottom row: therefore we need horizontal lines to completely fill the frame. Element 2 (vertical lines) remains the same from top to bottom in each column.
24	(1)	One frame is the sum of the other two frames (in shape). The frame that is made up of the other two is shaded.
25	(2)	Each individual element appears twice only in either the rows or columns.
26	(3)	The following principle applies either across the rows or down the columns: Dots on the outside of the box cancel out the dots on the inside of the box. Where dots are of the same category we add them eg Left column: 3 dots outside + 2 dots outside = 5 dots outside. Where the dots are in different categories we subtract them eg Middle column: 4 dots inside - 1 dot outside = 3 dots inside. Therefore our answer needs 2 dots on the outside
27	(2)	Each element appears twice only across each row or down each column.
28	(8)	Moving from left column to right column, the left frame is inverted horizontally (mirror image) to make the middle frame. The "flap" or right hand side of the shape is then removed to make the shape in the right column.
29	(6)	Looking at the top row and moving left to right, the curved horizontal lines in the left column become straight vertical lines in the middle column. In the third column the figure is rotated by 90 degrees and the straight lines become curved again and move back to their original position. The same principle applies in the other 2 rows.
30	(4)	Going down each column, add the top item to the centre item. Where there is the same kind of dot (filled or empty) in the same vertical position on BOTH sides of the line they cancel each other out. The result is the bottom item. The same is true going across each row.
31	(1)	Look at the foreground shapes first. Going from left to right along each row: Left frame + Middle frame = Right frame. Looking at the background elements and going from top to bottom down each row: Top frame + Middle frame = Bottom frame.
32	(3)	Left + Middle = Right Top + Middle = Bottom

33	(4)	You can look at this in either rows or columns. For example in each column as you move left to right two specific dots are being taken away. The position is the same for each frame.
34	(7)	Element "black dot" moves anticlockwise from left to right in each column. Element "white dot" is always opposite the black dot. Element "2 shaded dots" alternately moves apart and comes together to overlap. When they move apart they also rotate 90 degrees. Where no shaded dots are visible, it is because they are underneath the black and white dots.
35	(5)	Same "outside" shape in each column. The triangle is the only inside shape that has not appeared in each row or column.
36	(3)	Elements are shaded arc and clear arc. They start from opposite sides in the left column, overlap in the middle column, and cross over to form a solid oval shape - half clear - half shaded, in the right column.
37	(7)	Each element appears twice only across each row or down each column.
38	(5)	Each row or column has a 2-sided shape, a 3-sided shape and a 4-sided shape. Each row or column has a shape with all straight lines, a shape with all curved lines and a shape with both straight and curved lines. Two shapes in each row or column must have a base line.
39	(4)	In each row or column one frame is the sum of the other two.
40	(3)	Going from left to right across each row, the Left frame + the Middle frame = Right frame.

Abstract Reasoning

Question	Answer and explanation.
1	(B) Pattern runs the same every second frame. 1 –3 –5 etc.
2	(C) Pattern runs the same every second frame. 1 –3 –5 etc.
3	(A) A single line is being added to each frame so the fifth frame must have 5 lines in it.
4	(E) Pattern runs the same every second frame. 1 –3 –5 etc.
5	(A) Pattern runs the same every second frame. 1 –3 –5 etc.
6	(D) Pattern runs the same every second frame. 1 –3 –5 etc.
7	(D) Developmental: a limb is being added to the body in a particular order & thin/thick body line.
8	(E) Developmental: each frame has one clear dot with a shaded dot being added to each frame, so therefore we need four shaded dots with one clear dot.
9	(A) There are two elements in this matrix, both doing their own thing. The bar alternates from shaded to un-shaded, from left diagonal to right diagonal. The fifth frame needs to be a left diagonal that is shaded…...that leaves A, C or D. The star moves in the following sequence: top, bottom, bottom and then top, so the star in the fifth frame would need to be at the bottom.
10	(B) This pattern is commonly called a 'boomerang' because it reaches a peak in its progression and then returns to its original starting point. Notice : 1– 2 –3—2 –1.
11	(E) The triangle is rotating anticlockwise - 45 degrees after each frame.
12	(A) Starting from the first frame, a new shape is being added to each frame as we move along. Each shape remains in its original position.
13	(C) Each shape is divided into an increasing number of segments. Example 2, 3, 4, 5, 6.
14	(C) The vertical lines running along the horizontal line are moving in opposite directions and at the same time they are shifting from top to bottom.

15	(B)	There are 3 elements in these frames all doing their own thing. Firstly the 'horse shoe' is rotating anticlockwise 90 degrees. Secondly the shading runs consecutively clear—dark—clear—dark, etc. Thirdly the dot runs along the frames, middle—top—bottom—middle—top.
16	(B)	The vertical arrow is pointing down, down, then up and up again, so the next one would have to be pointing down. The horizontal arrow is alternating left, right, left, right....so the next one would have to be left.
17	(A)	The vertical lines are alternating from double to single across the frames. The black dot is alternating from left to right either side of the vertical line(s). The black dot is also moving from a top position, to a middle position and to a bottom position within each frame as it progresses.
18	(C)	This is the 'boomerang' principle in action. See Question 10.
19	(C)	The pattern consists of a shape with substance, that is the ends join up to give it a specific shape. This alternates with a single line where there is an end and a beginning.
20	(D)	Firstly a new shape is being added to each frame e.g.: 2—3—4—5 etc. Secondly each alternate frame has one black dot appearing.
21	(E)	Each shape evolves with an extra line being added. Example 3—4—5—6—etc.
22	(B)	Firstly the circle alternates from small to big to small to big. Secondly the line alternates from horizontal to vertical to horizontal to vertical. Thirdly the line is moving across the frames from top to middle to bottom back to middle — so the line would have to be horizontal and positioned at the top.
23	(B)	Pattern runs the same every second frame. 1 –3 –5 etc.
24	(C)	Pattern runs the same every second frame. 1 –3 –5 etc.

Mechanical Reasoning 1

Q1 Wheels W and X are each 6 centimetres across. Wheels Y and Z are each 3 centimetres across. When W makes one complete turn, Z will make

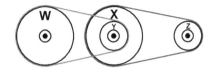

D **Four complete turns**

The ratio between wheels W, X and Y, Z is 2:1. Therefore when wheel W turns once, wheel Y will turn twice, and since wheel Y is driving wheel X, wheel X will turn twice and wheel Z will rotate 4 times as it is half the size of wheel X.

Q2 If handle A is pushed upwards in the direction of the arrow

B **end C will move up and end B will move down**

View animation at www.paragontraining.com.au/msar

Q3 If wheel W turns clockwise as indicated by the arrow, Z will

D **move to and fro**

OSCILLATE - swing to and fro; vary between extremes.

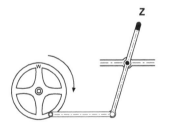

Q4 If wheel A turns anticlockwise as indicated by the arrow, D will

D **jam the mechanism**

The teeth are interlocked with opposing forces. Principle of mechanics: interlocked wheels will always alternate clockwise - anticlockwise - clockwise etc. OR vice versa.

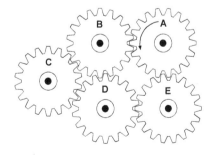

Q5 A and B are blocks attached to the cord which runs around this vertical system of wheels. If the cord is pulled to the left, as indicated by the arrow, how will A and B move?

B   **A goes down and B to the right**

View animation at www.paragontraining.com.au/msar

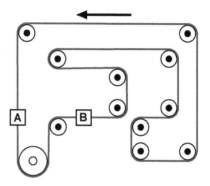

Q6 If handle H is pulled down, as indicated by the arrow, how will the hook at the end of non-fixed pivot L move?

C   **hook will move left but remain the same distance from L**

View animation at www.paragontraining.com.au/msar

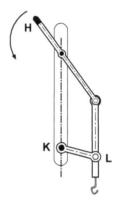

Q7 If handle A is pulled down, as indicated by the arrow, how will B move?

C   **B will move to the right and up**

View animation at www.paragontraining.com.au/msar

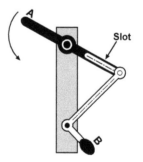

Q8 Wheel Z turns anticlockwise, as shown by the arrow, and drives wheel Y. A connecting rod attached to wheel Y moves in a slot. Will non fixed pivot P move

D   **to and fro continuously**

View animation at www.paragontraining.com.au/msar

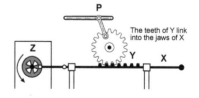

Q9 In this 5-storey factory, the motor on the ground floor uses belts A, B, C and D to drive conveyors on the 1st, 2nd, 3rd and 4th floors. If the conveyors on the 1st and 2nd floors are turning but the conveyors on the 3rd and 4th floors are not, which of the belts is most likely to have broken?

C   C

View animation at www.paragontraining.com.au/msar

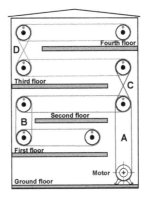

Q10 If handle X is pulled down as indicated by the arrow, Z (hook) will

A   move left and closer to Y

View animation at www.paragontraining.com.au/msar

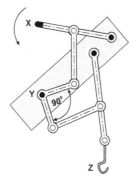

Q11 If handle X is pulled down, as indicated by the arrow, W (hook) will

D   move left and further away from Z

View animation at www.paragontraining.com.au/msar

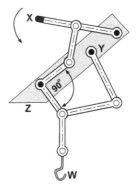

Q12 If handle A is pulled down as indicated by the arrow, B will move

B   down and further away from pivot Y

View animation at www.paragontraining.com.au/msar

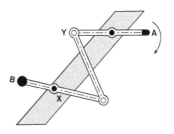

Q13 If wheels X and Y move in the direction of the arrows, A will

C **not move at all as the mechanism would jam**

Teeth are interlocked with opposing forces.

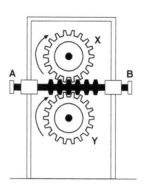

Q14 If the belt driven by the motor is travelling anticlockwise as shown by the arrow, then how many wheels in total will be turning clockwise?

B **Two**

Principle of mechanics: crossover on wheel A to B and C to D changes direction of rotation.

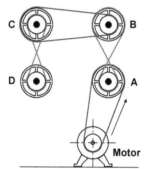

Q15 Wheels B and C have pins which fit into the slots in wheel A. Both wheels B and C turn in the direction of the arrows and drive wheel A.

Wheel A will

D **not operate as C and B are opposing forces**

View animation at www.paragontraining.com.au/msar

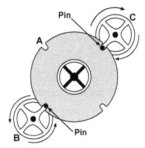

Q16 Block A is supported by springs X and Z. Spring Z is three times as strong as spring X. If both screws are turned at the same speed in the directions shown by the arrows, towards which point will block A move?

B **Y**

Equal rotations of each screw move the block upwards and left equally. The motion is independent of the strength of the spring, but the lower screw will need more force. The block therefore moves towards Y.

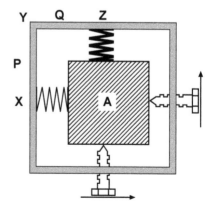

Q17 If wheel A turns in the direction as shown by the arrow, which one of the following is true?

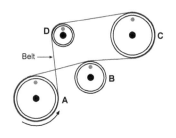

C **A and B turn in the same direction**

View animation at www.paragontraining.com.au/msar

Q18 X and Y are blocks attached to the cord which runs around this system of wheels. If the cord is pulled in the direction of the arrow until each block passes its first wheel, then which of the following is true?

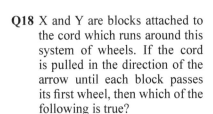
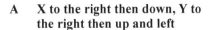

A **X to the right then down, Y to the right then up and left**

View animation at www.paragontraining.com.au/msar

Q19 Wheels X, Y and Z can turn to and fro. If Z is turned clockwise, as shown by the arrow, then

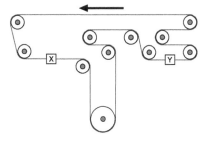
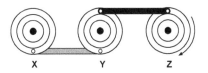

A **X and Y will both turn clockwise**

View animation at www.paragontraining.com.au/msar

Q20 If handle J is pulled up, as shown by the arrow, how will M (hook) move?

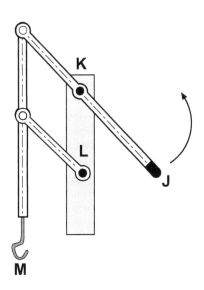

C **down to the left, further away from L**

View animation at www.paragontraining.com.au/msar

Q21 A, B and C are gears which turn on shafts and drive rods X and Y. When wheels A and C turn clockwise as shown by the arrows, rods X and Y will

A **slide in opposite directions to each other**

View animation at www.paragontraining.com.au/msar

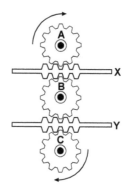

Q22 If the handle is pulled to the right as shown by the arrow, T will move

D **closer to the handle, same distance from R**

View animation at www.paragontraining.com.au/msar

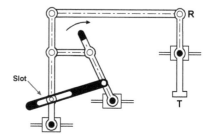

Q23 If the belt driven by the motor travels anti-clockwise as shown by the arrow, then which of the following is true?

A **M and K turn in opposite directions and J and L turn in opposite directions**

View animation at www.paragontraining.com.au/msar

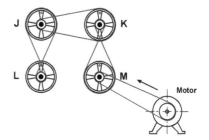

Q24 If the handle is pulled in the direction of the arrow, which mechanism out of J, K, L and M will act as a brake?

C **L**

View animation at www.paragontraining.com.au/msar

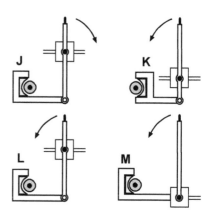

Q25 When S turns anticlockwise as shown by the arrow, it will drive wheels T and U

D **Wheel T turns clockwise and U turns anticlockwise, to and fro**

View animation at www.paragontraining.com.au/msar

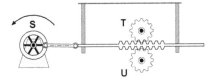

Q26 When handle S is pulled to the right as shown by the arrow, T will

C **move closer to V, same distance from U**

View animation at www.paragontraining.com.au/msar

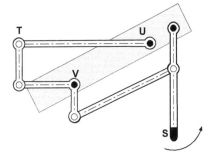

Q27 When the motor drives wheels L, K and M, which one of the following statements is true?

B **not work because L and M are opposing forces**

View animation at www.paragontraining.com.au/msar

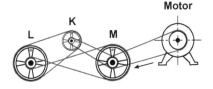

Q28 Wheel A has a pin near its edge. The pin engages in the slot in wheel B. When wheel A turns clockwise as shown, how will wheel B move?

B **anticlockwise intermittently**

View animation at www.paragontraining.com.au/msar

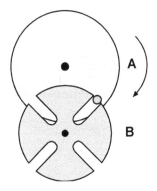

Q29 Wheels J and L turn as indicated by the arrows. Which of the following statements is true?

B   all wheels turn anticlockwise except for M and L

View animation at www.paragontraining.com.au/msar

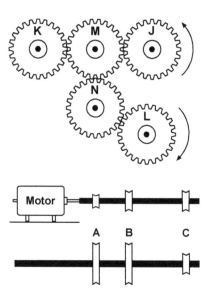

Q30 The motor drives the upper shaft at a constant speed. A, B and C are pairs of wheels attached to each shaft. To make the lower shaft turn the fastest, around which pair of wheels would a belt be attached?

D   C

With the belt in position A it takes 3 rotations of the top shaft to make the lower shaft rotate once. In position B it takes 3 rotations of the top shaft to make the lower shaft rotate twice. In position C the top and bottom shafts rotate at the same speed.

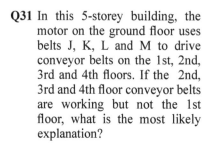

Q31 In this 5-storey building, the motor on the ground floor uses belts J, K, L and M to drive conveyor belts on the 1st, 2nd, 3rd and 4th floors. If the 2nd, 3rd and 4th floor conveyor belts are working but not the 1st floor, what is the most likely explanation?

B   belt K is broken

View animation at www.paragontraining.com.au/msar

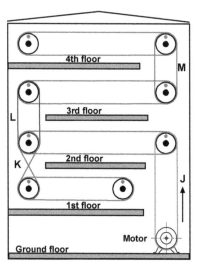

Q32 Cam A turns clockwise at constant speed, and drives punch P through the levers shown. For each rotation of the cam, punch P will

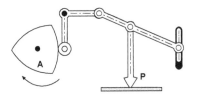

B **punch onto the plate three times**

The cam is three sided so it will operate the punch three times per revolution. The cam follower is shown in its lowest position where the punch is touching the plate so it can never punch through the plate.

Mechanical Reasoning 2

Q1 As pin P is hammered down, the fit of axle A to wheel W will become:

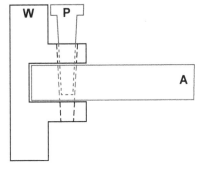

A **tighter**

The pin and holes are tapered (wider at the top than the bottom) so the fit will get better as the pin is hammered down and the joint will become tighter.

Q2 Identical floats have equal lead weights attached as shown. They are released into the liquids shown. After the floats come to rest, which container has the highest level of liquid?

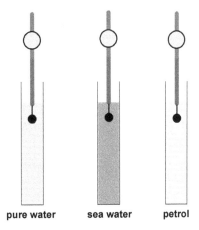

pure water   sea water   petrol

A **petrol**

Archimedes Principle applies to this question. An object floats when it displaces an amount of liquid equal to its own weight. Petrol is the least dense liquid so more must be displaced for the float to float. It therefore rises the most.

Q3 Weight W is placed on a plank which is supported by scales A and B. As W is moved from right to left along the plank, what will happen to the scale readings?

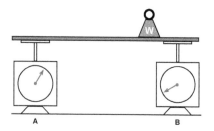

C   A will increase and B will decrease

At all times the total weight shown by the two scales is equal to the weight of the plank plus the weight of W. As the weight moves from right to left, more weight is taken by the left balance so A increases and B decreases. The scales show the same weight when W is half way across.

Q4 Which wheel will rotate the fastest?

Driven

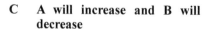

D   all the same

View animation at www.paragontraining.com.au/msar

Q5 At which point is the pressure greatest?

B   B

The pressure of a column of liquid depends only on the difference in height between the top and the bottom. This is why divers have to take care the deeper they dive as more pressure is placed on the body.

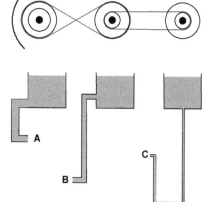

Q6 Which tree will fall to the right?

A   A

The tree falls when its centre of gravity (COG) overhangs the base of the tree. If pushed in the direction of the small cut, the lower trunk supports the upper trunk before the COG hangs over.

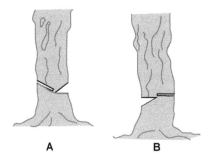

Q7 Which pendulum swings the fastest?

C   C

The time for a complete swing of a pendulum depends on the length of the string, but not on the weight of the bob.

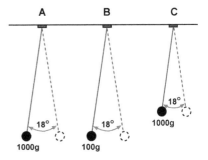

Q8 Wheel A is driven clockwise as shown. Which of the following statements is true?

D   wheel B will rotate to and fro

This motion is called "oscillation". Oscillation means moving to and fro.

Q9 Which switch or switches must be closed to light both globes?

A   A only

There has to be an unbroken path between the battery and the lamp(s) for them to light.

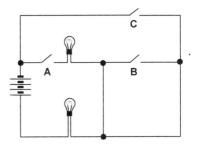

Q10 When cams X, Y and Z are driven about their fixed pivots, which rod will travel the greatest distance?

C   C

The cam that has the greatest distance between the pivot point and the centre of the cam causes the greatest movement in the rod.

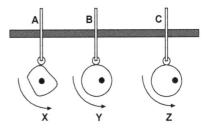

Q11 In this circuit which of the following statements is false?

C **operating both switches together can light the lamp**

There has to be an unbroken path between the battery and the lamp(s) for them to light. This circuit is used for lighting the landing of a two storey house.

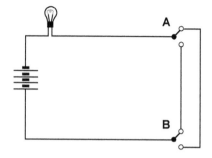

Q12 Which pair or pairs of magnets will attract?

C **A and C**

Like poles repel and unlike poles attract.

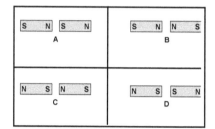

Q13 The circular glass tube is filled with liquid and heated from below as shown. Which of the following statements is true?

A **the liquid will start to move either clockwise or anticlockwise at random**

Hot liquids are less dense than cold liquids so they rise. If the circular tube is heated in the centre, as shown, you can't predict in which direction the liquid will go round. However, if the flame was off centre, the liquid would always go round in one direction.

Q14 Shaft S is rotated clockwise as shown. Which of the following statements is true?

A **A turns anti-clockwise and B turns clockwise**

View animation to understand this mechanism.

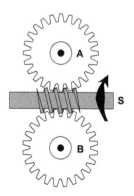

Q15 Each group of pulleys has wheels whose diameters are in the ratio 1:2:3. The top pulley wheels are all driven at the same speed of rotation. Which wheel will rotate the fastest?

A   A

Watch the counters to see the different ratios between wheels after the drive wheel turns a complete revolution.

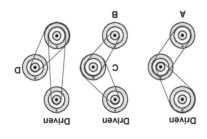

Q16 Pulley A turns clockwise as shown. Which of the following statements is true?

C   the same number of pulleys turn clockwise as anticlockwise

View animation at www.paragontraining.com.au/msar

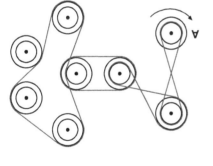

Q17 Which tyre has been used under-inflated?

C   C

View animation at www.paragontraining.com.au/msar

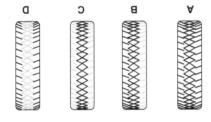

Q18 The circular plate is free to rotate around fixed pivot P. Three fixed threaded holes are in the plate below. In which hole should thumbscrew T be placed to give the circular plate the maximum possible movement?

D   either A or B

When the thumbscrew is placed in either A or B, the plate can move the full length of the curved slot. When the thumbscrew is placed in position C (the straight slot), the plate can move only a very small amount.

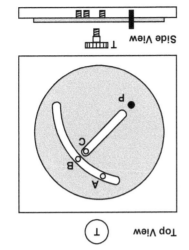

Top View

Side View

Q19 Rack A is pushed in the direction shown by the arrow. Which of the following statements is true?

D   rack B does not move

Rack A and gears X and Y form a three gear interlocking system which cannot move. Therefore rack B can't move either.

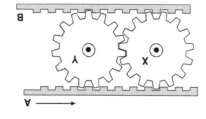

Q20 A spring holds lever L against fixed pin P. Gear X drives gear Y. Which of the following statements is true?

B   with a weak spring, gear X can turn anticlockwise

Pin P stops lever L from being pushed down. Therefore Y can't move anticlockwise and X can't move clockwise. With a weak spring gear Y can push the lever up when it turns clockwise and so X can turn anticlockwise.

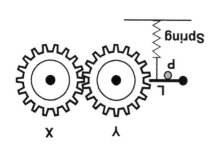